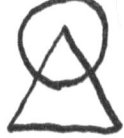

A PRACTICAL MANIFESTO FOR CREATIVITY

JOHN F GERRARD

COPYRIGHT © 2021

ALL RIGHTS RESERVED

EDITED BY JIM KEVLIN

ISBN: 9798752003639

FOR
JEN

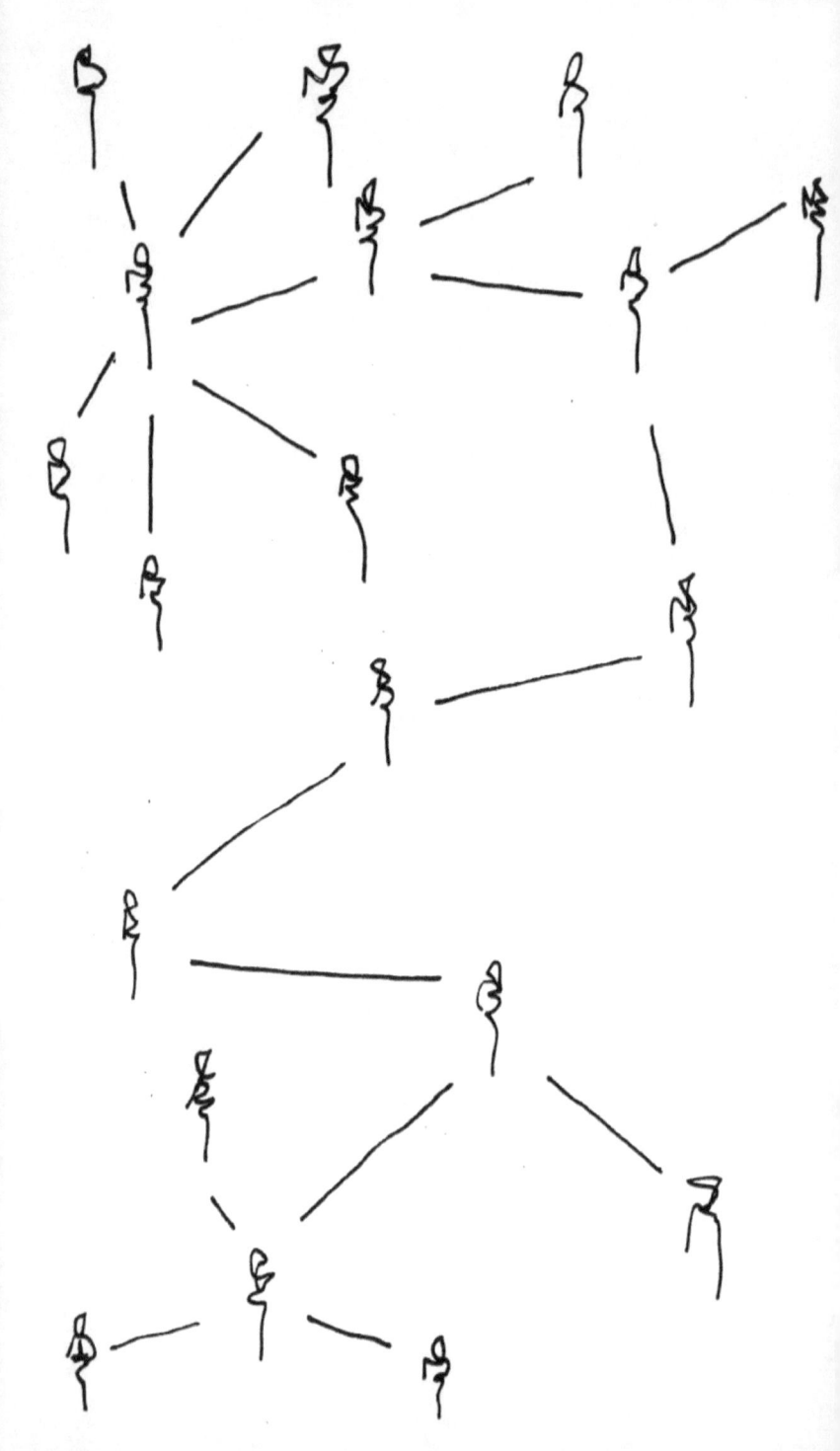

IDEA / MATERIAL

INTERACTION ISSUE

MATERIAL / IDEA

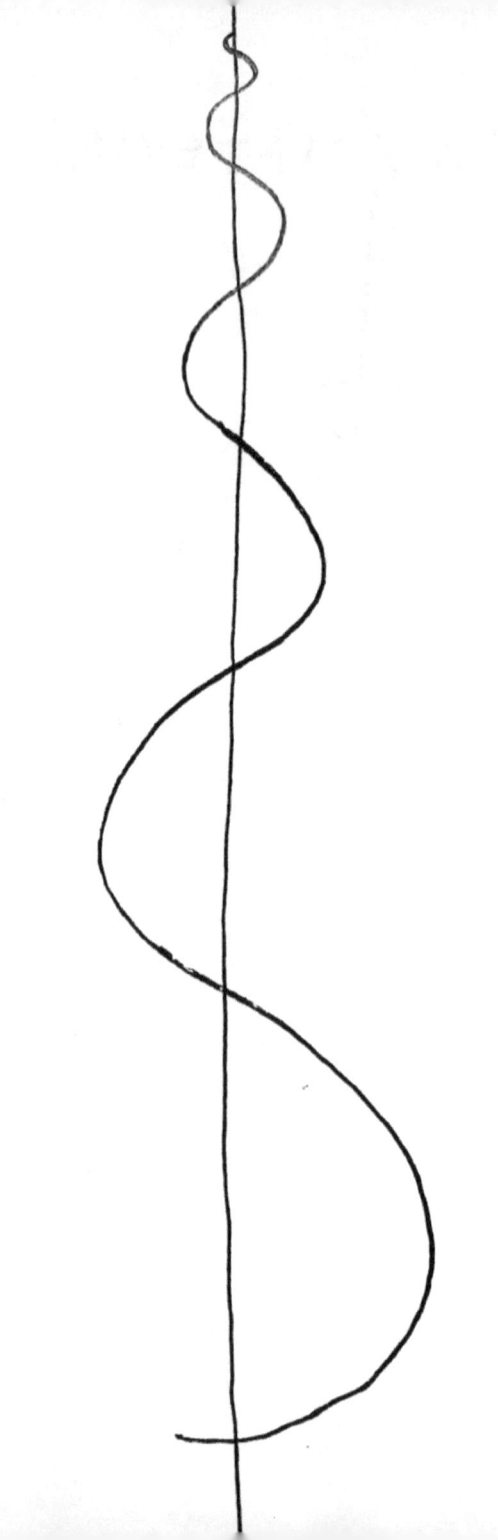

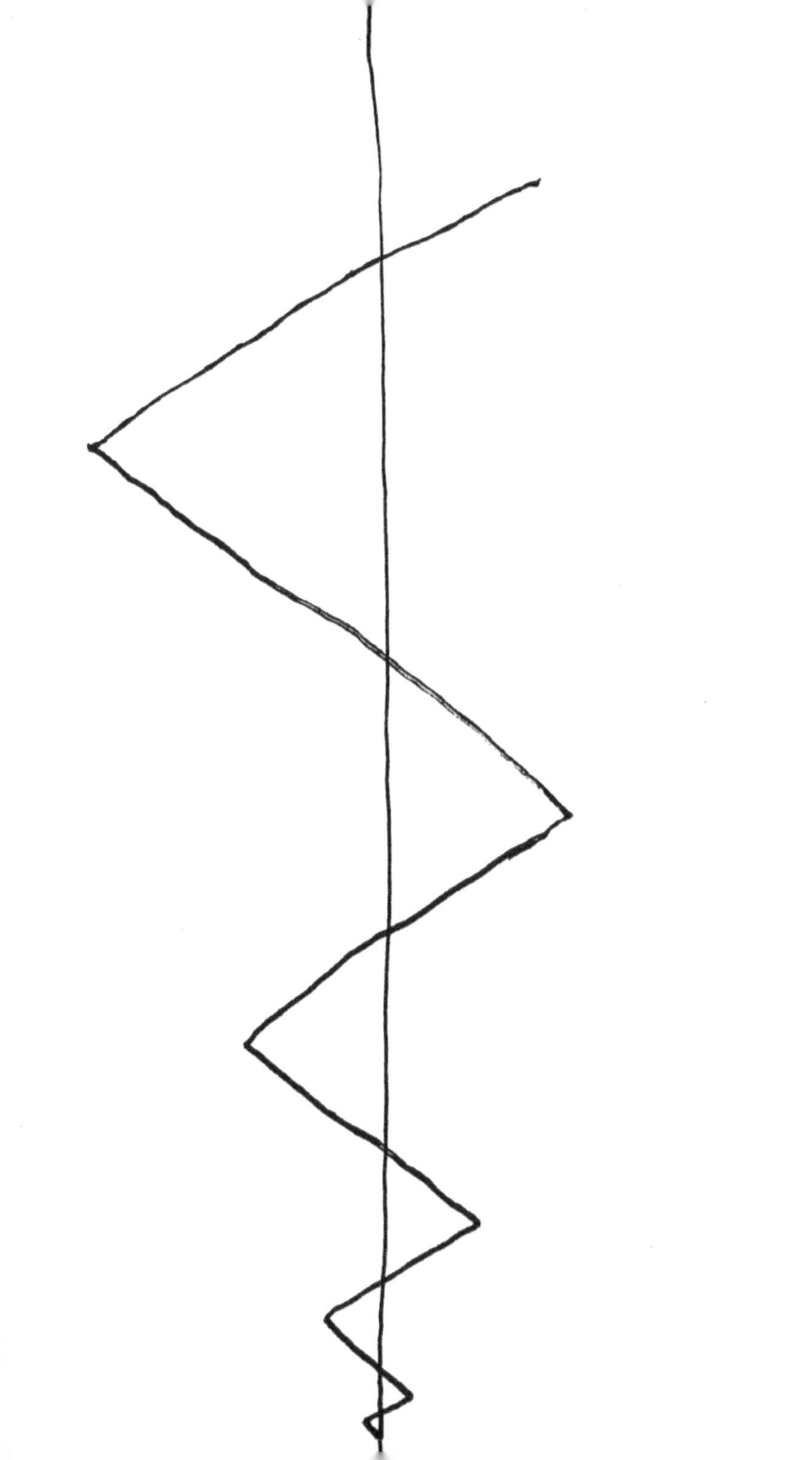

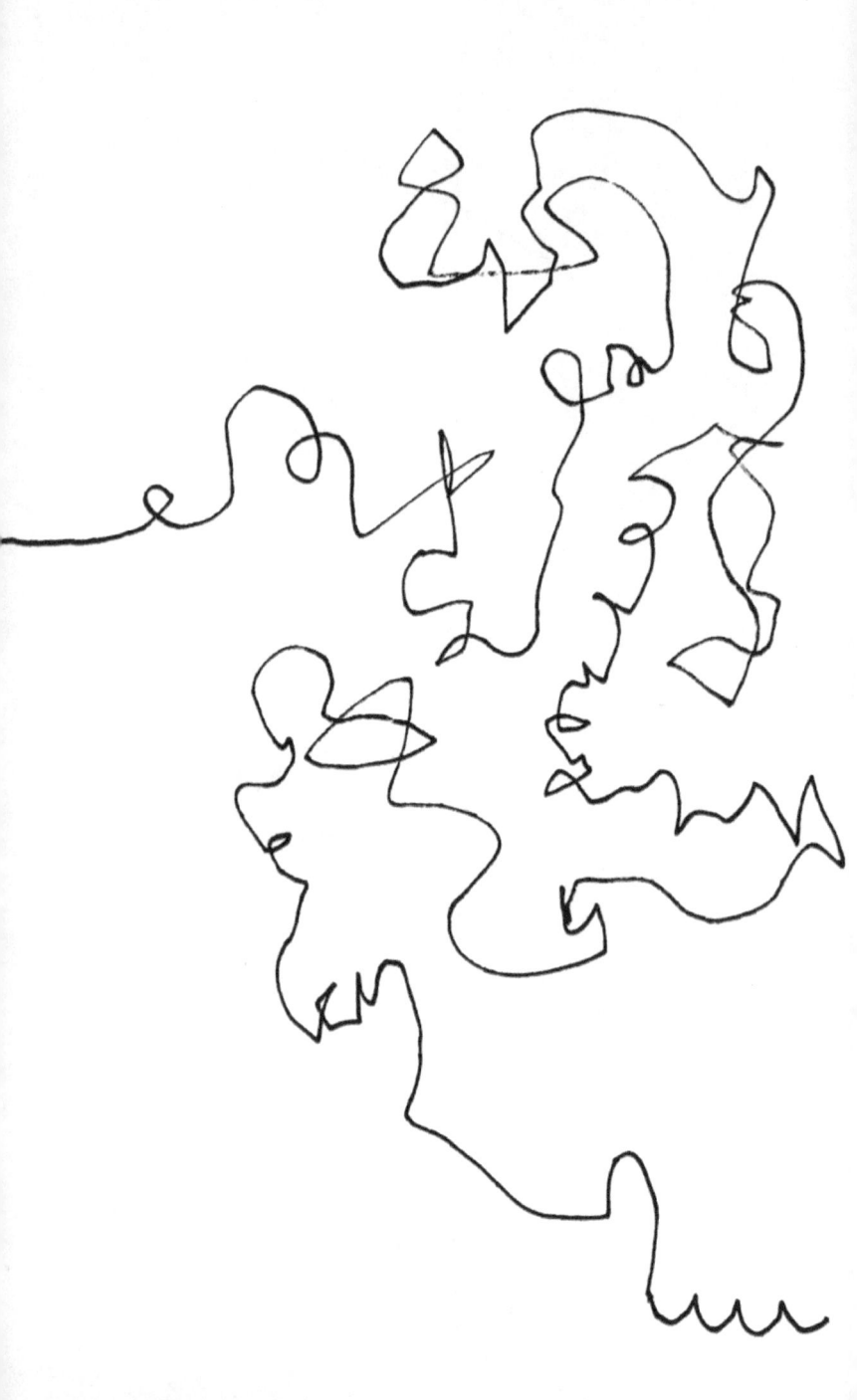

1.1

FIND A CREATIVE PROCESS YOU ENJOY. IF YOU HAVE A PROCESS THAT YOU ENJOY, YOU WON'T MIND PRACTISING AND UNPLEASANT RESULTS WON'T MATTER AS MUCH.

DRAWN WHILE LISTENING TO
ASHA JEFFERIES
WITH MY EYES
CLOSED.

1.2

YOU DON'T ALWAYS NEED A FINISHED PRODUCT FOR CREATIVITY TO BE WORTHWHILE. PLAY IS AN IMPORTANT ACTIVITY IN ITSELF.

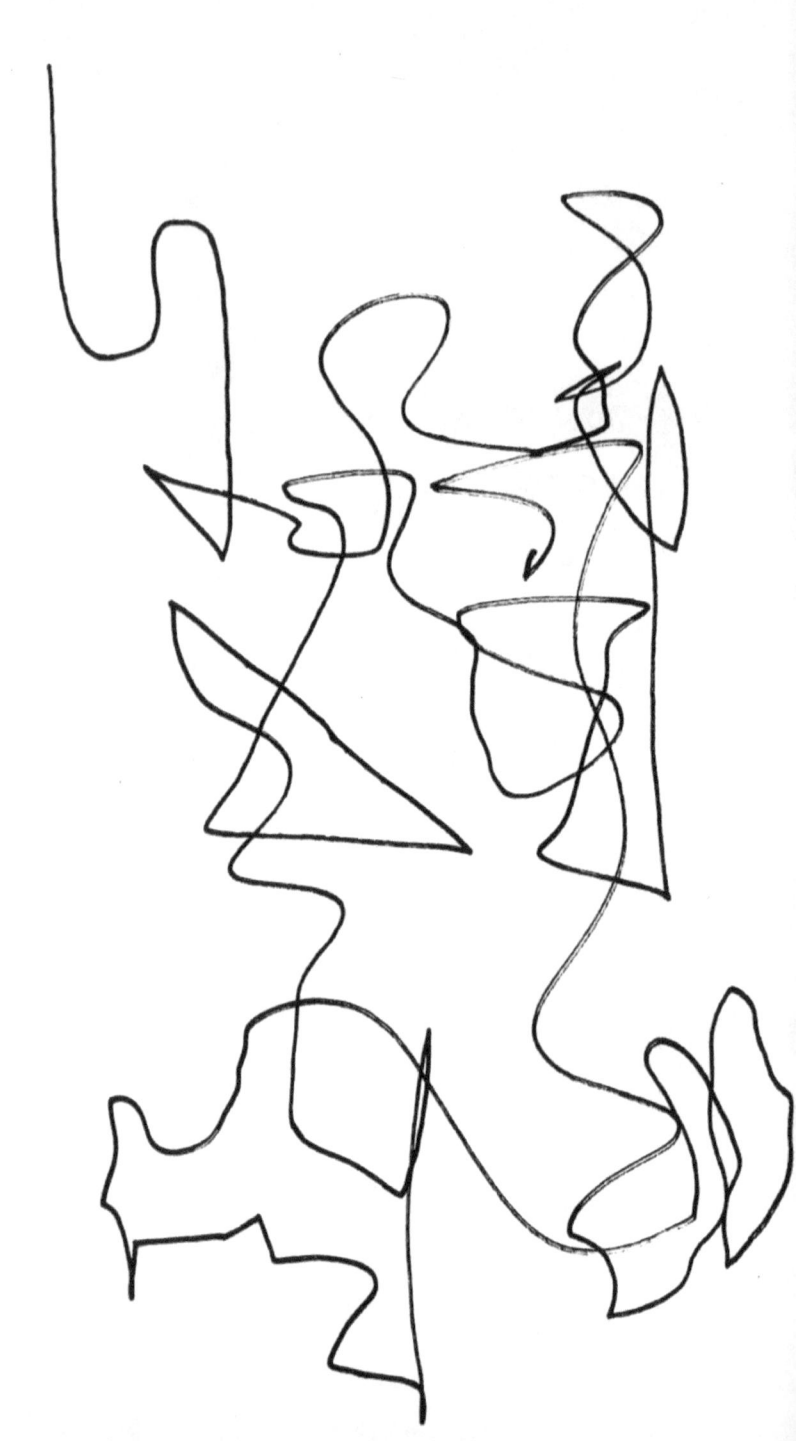

1.3

Good art could be seen to be art that succeeds in realizing the artist's intentions. By this logic, if your goal is to evoke a certain feeling and you do, you have succeeded.

If your goal is to be free from goals and realizing intentions, you can't lose.

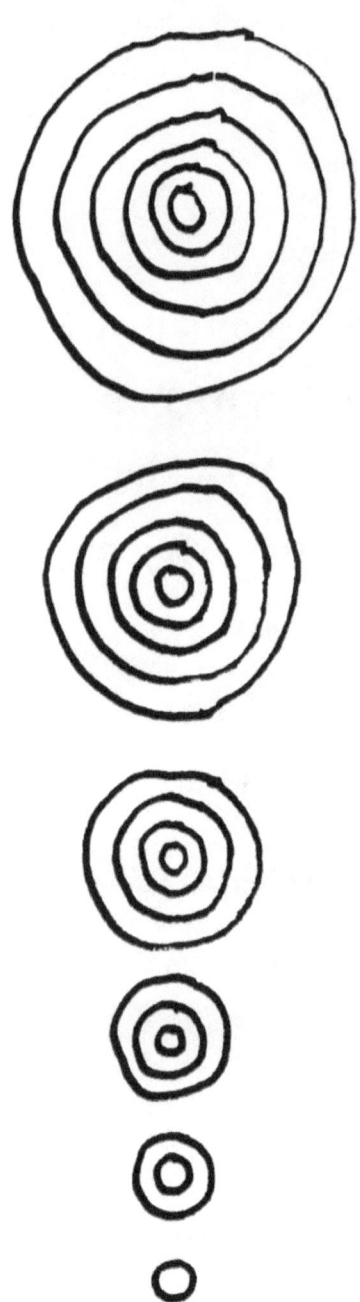

1.4

CREATIVITY IS A MUSCLE. IT TAKES TIME TO STRENGTHEN THAT MUSCLE SO YOUR ABILITY MATCHES WHAT YOU FIND WORTHWHILE TO MAKE. DON'T GET DISCOURAGED IF WHAT YOU MAKE IN THE BEGINNING DOESN'T MATCH WHAT YOU THINK IS GOOD.

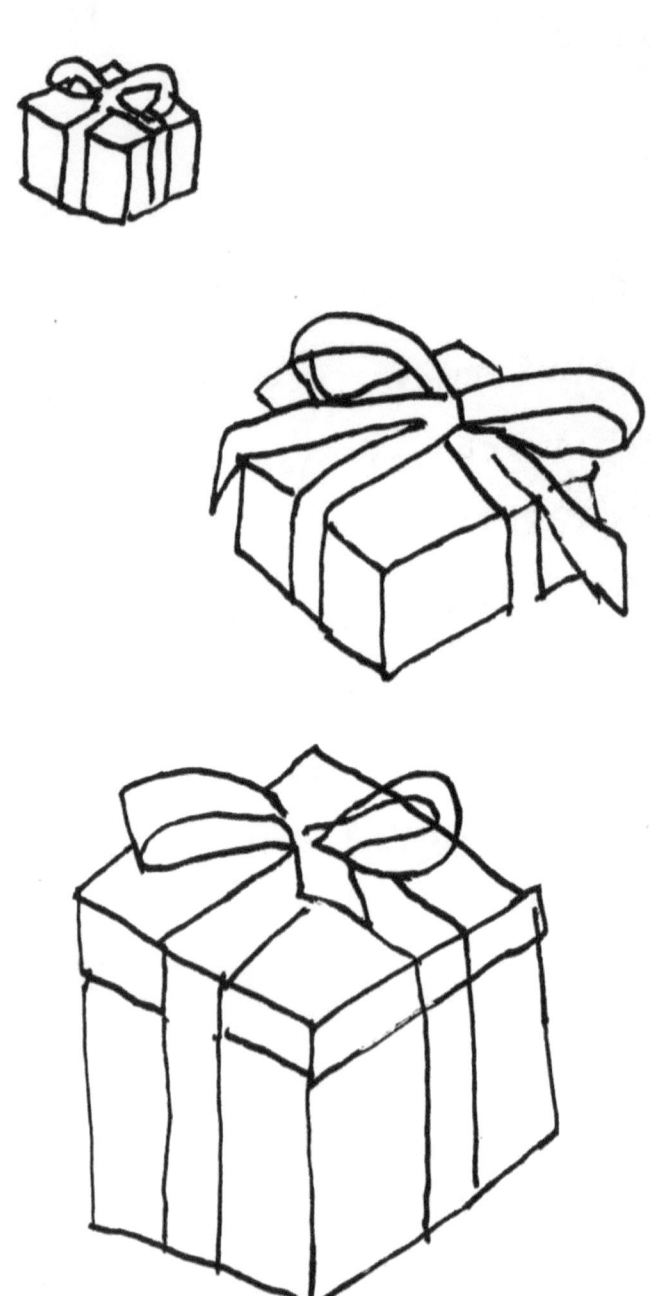

1.5

IT ISN'T NECESSARY TO VIEW THE WORK FROM AN INTELLECTUAL ANGLE. MAYBE YOU'RE WORKING INTUITIVELY AND ARE MAKING THINGS THAT FEEL RIGHT.
WHY THINGS FEEL RIGHT IS OFTEN MYSTERIOUS. SOMETIMES OUR HIDDEN INTENTIONS REVEAL THEMSELVES YEARS AFTER THE WORK IS MADE.

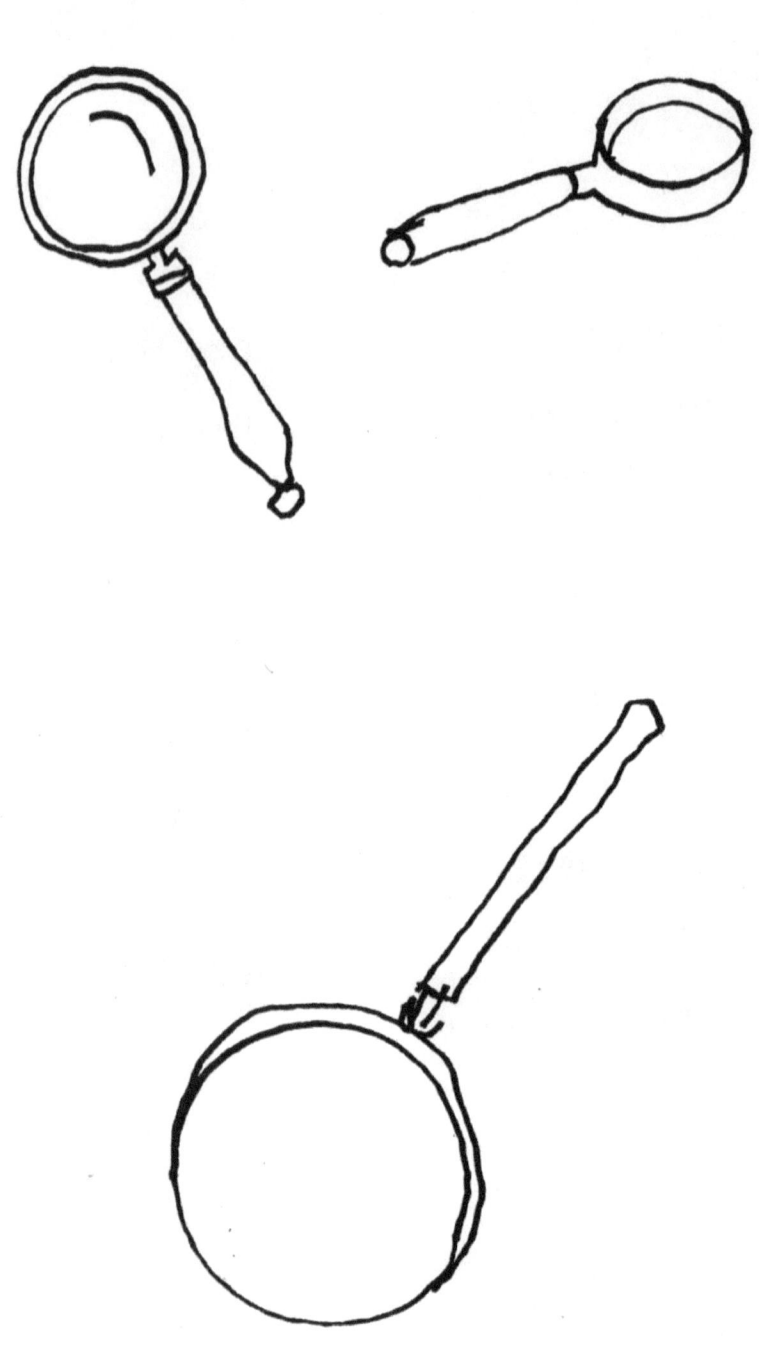

1.6

If you'd like to be constructively critical, it may be helpful to examine how the sense experience is serving your conceptual intentions. What are your goals regarding the message and/or philosophy of the work? What are the materials you're using "saying"? What sort of response does the work evoke?

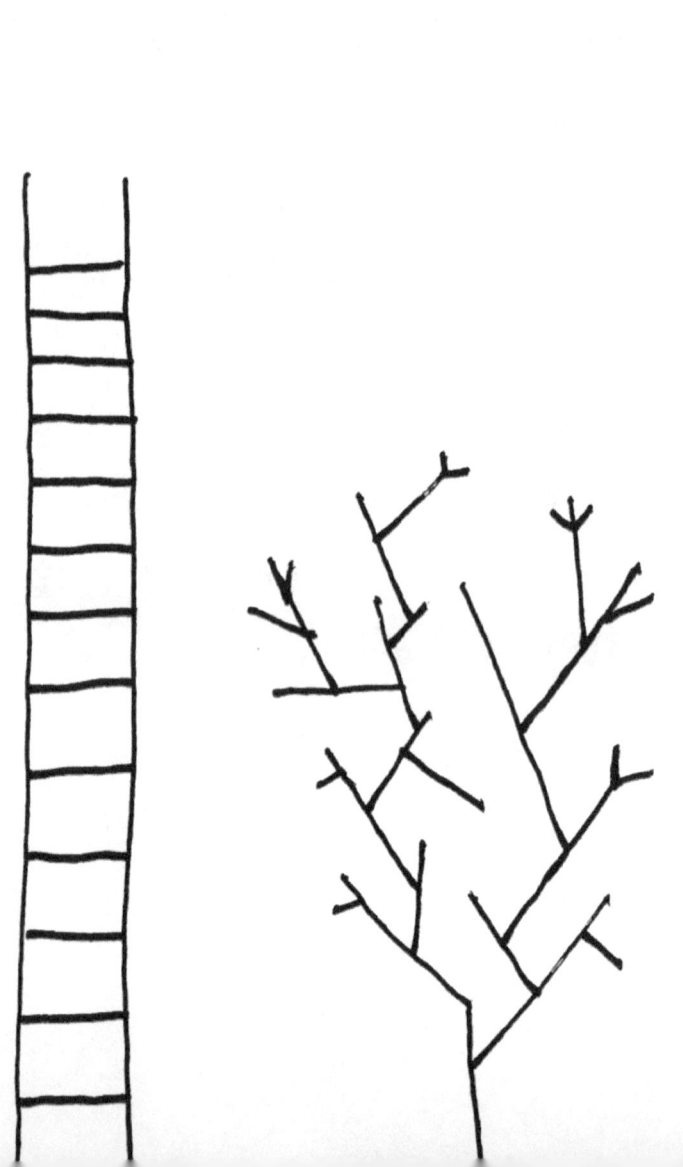

1.7

You may have an idea (conceptual) or physical image (sense data) you are working to represent, or you may work without knowing exactly where you're going, with each mark being a reaction to the ones before it.

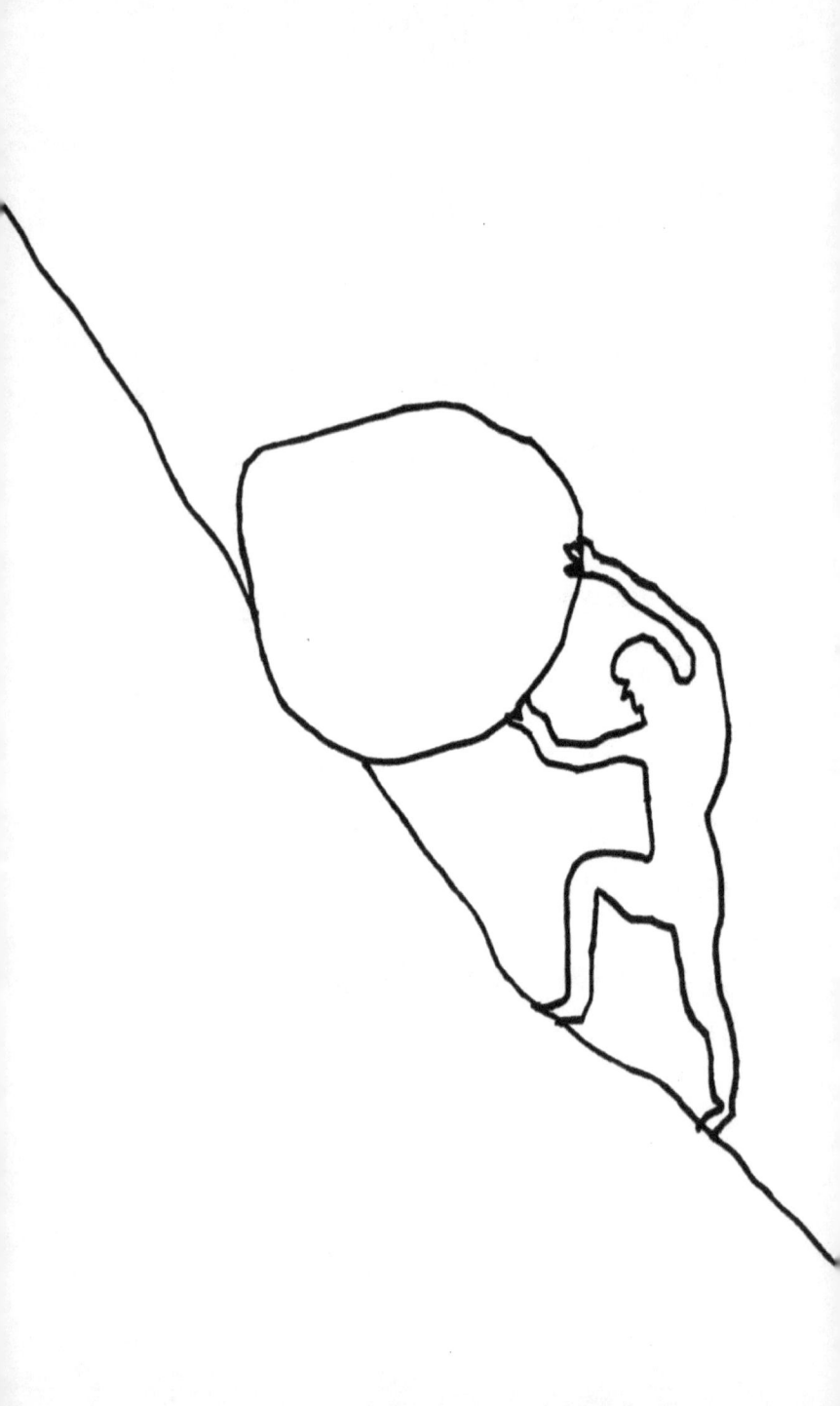

1.8

If you want to make products that better serve their goal, practise lots, but not in circles. Practise in a way that promotes growth and the desired evolution. Getting practical and honest feedback is an important part of this process if you wish for your creativity to resonate with others and to understand the effect it has on others. Every viewer brings their own set of values and biases to the work.

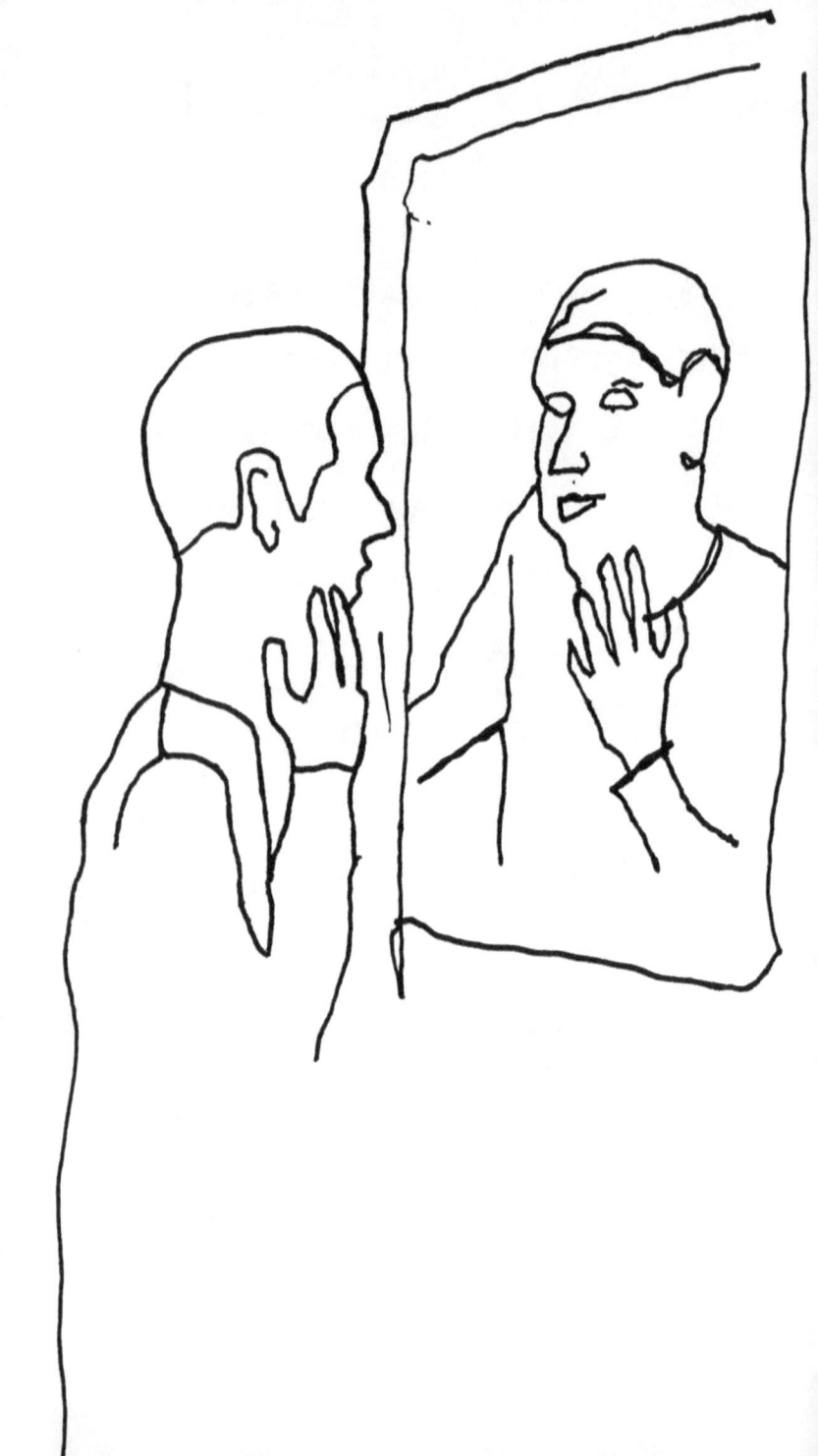

1.9

When we move towards our aspirations and values, we evolve. This is why being conscious of our values and motivations is important if we're to be informed enough to make the choices that move us towards what we find important. Creativity gives us something material to reflect with.

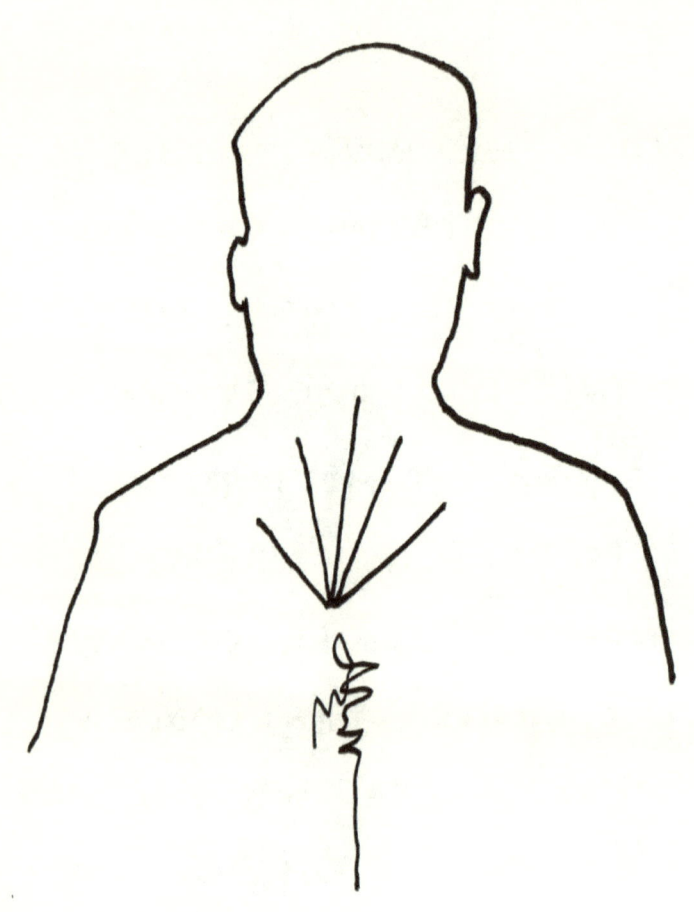

1.10

AS YOU FIND YOUR CREATIVE VOICE, YOU GET TO KNOW WHAT WAS ONCE A HIDDEN PART OF YOURSELF.

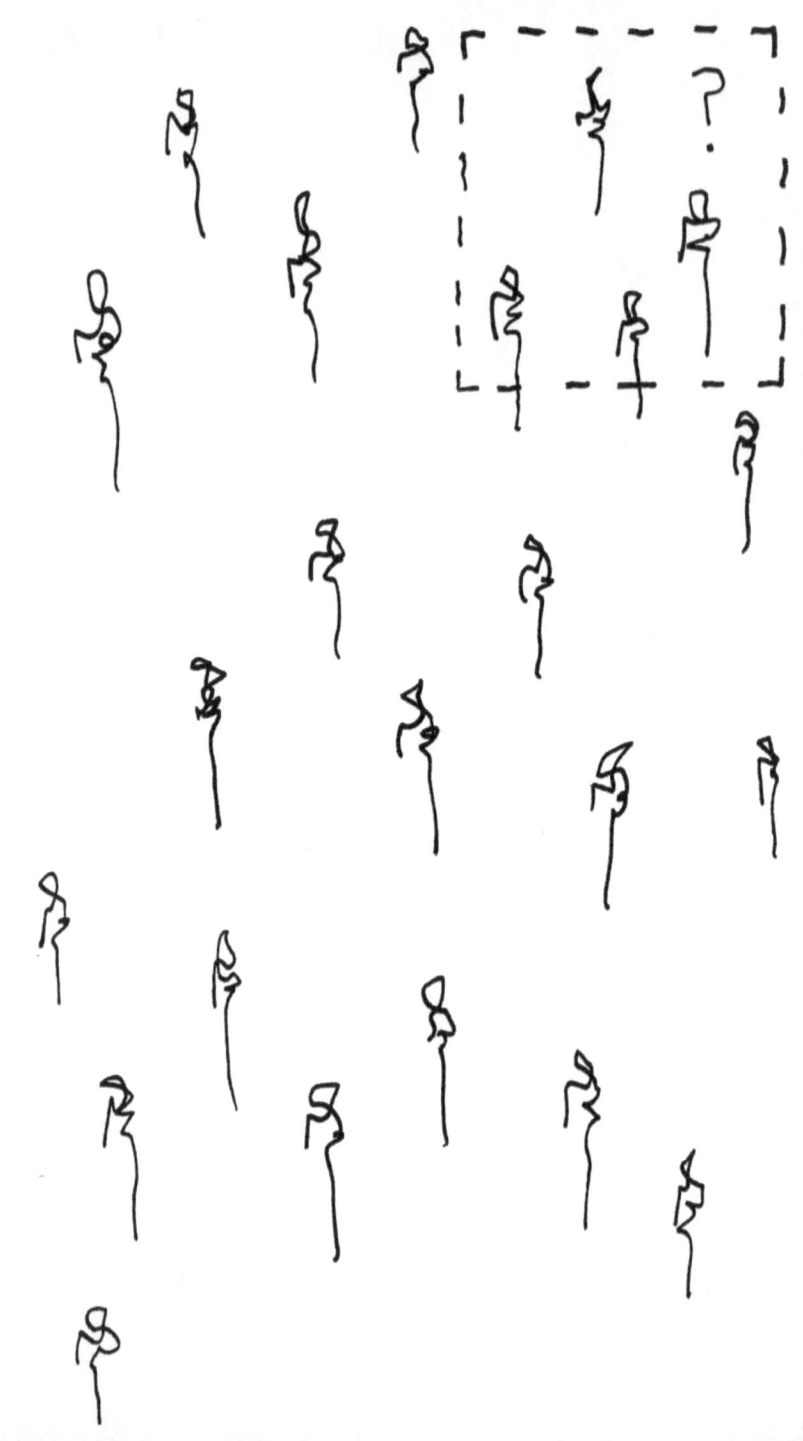

1.11

WHEN WE MAKE AN IMAGE, WE REVEAL AND DISTORT ASPECTS DEPENDING ON OUR DECISIONS. BY SEEING REMNANTS OF THOSE DECISIONS, WE CAN BECOME AWARE OF OUR DECISIONS. IF WE ARE AWARE OF OUR DECISIONS, WE ARE IN A POSITION TO CHANGE THEM. AN EXAMPLE OF AN ARTISTIC DECISION WOULD BE IN WHICH AREA OF YOUR VIEW YOU SELECT TO PHOTOGRAPH WHILE TAKING A PICTURE. YOU CAN ASK, WHY DID I HIGHLIGHT THAT ASPECT OF MY VIEW; WHY DID I LEAVE OTHER ASPECTS OUT? HOW WILL THIS INFORM MY NEXT PIECE OF WORK?

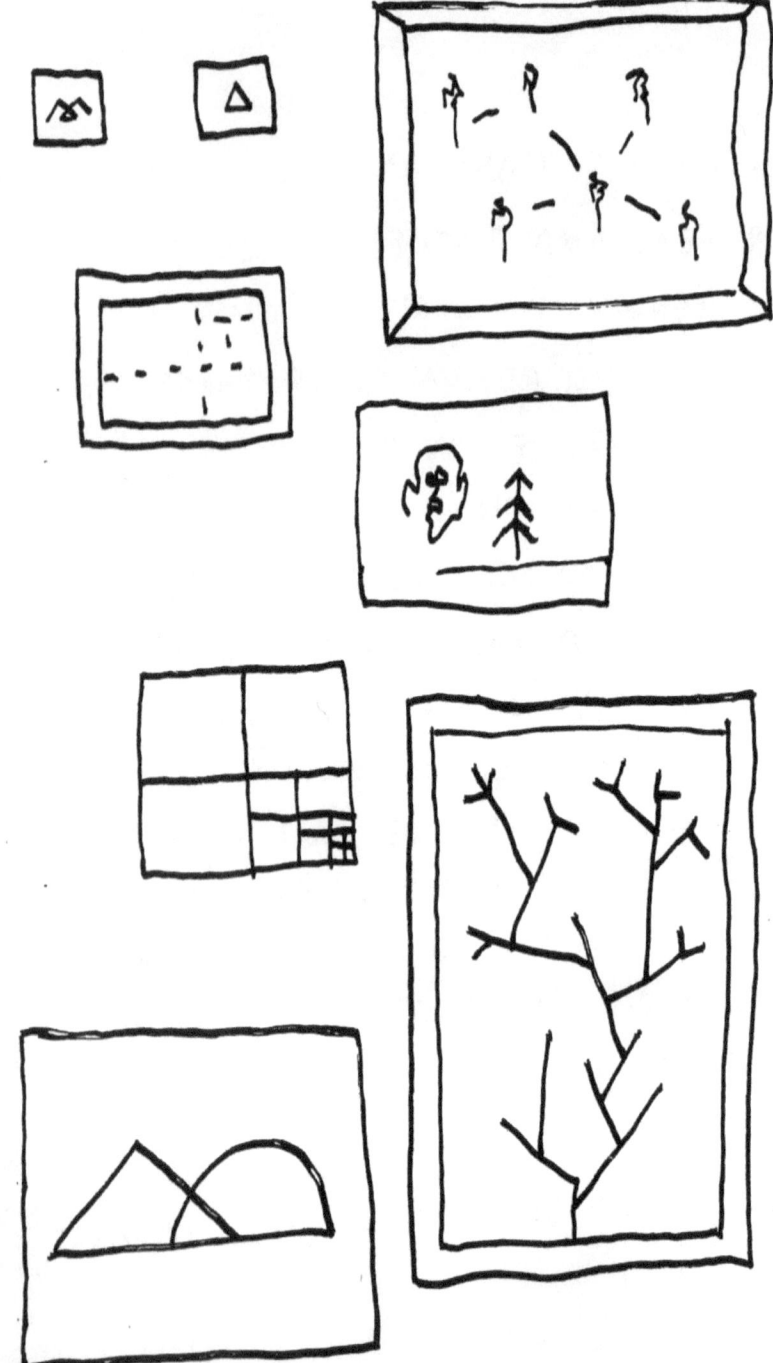

1.12

YOU WILL MAKE BETTER WORK BY HAVING A HISTORY OF YOUR WORK TO LEARN FROM.

QUICKLY DRAWN FIGURES
UNTIL COMPOSITION FELT
RIGHT.

1.13

There are rules you can follow that others have made, or rules you can make for yourself. Either way, you can follow or not follow the rules, as you choose.

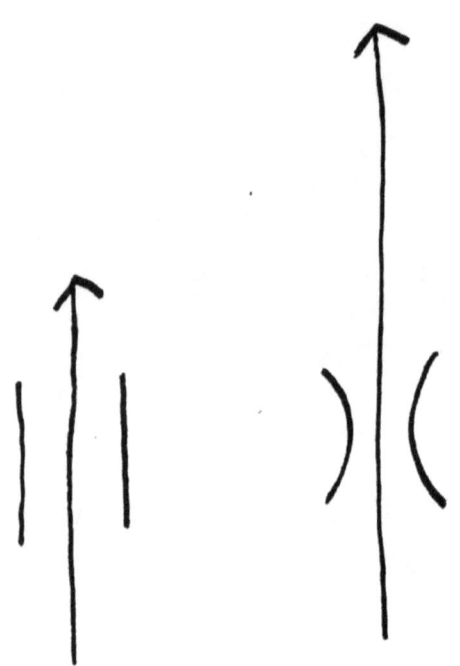

1.14

There is a certain freedom in restrictions. I'm reminded of a hose: when you make the opening smaller the water comes out stronger.

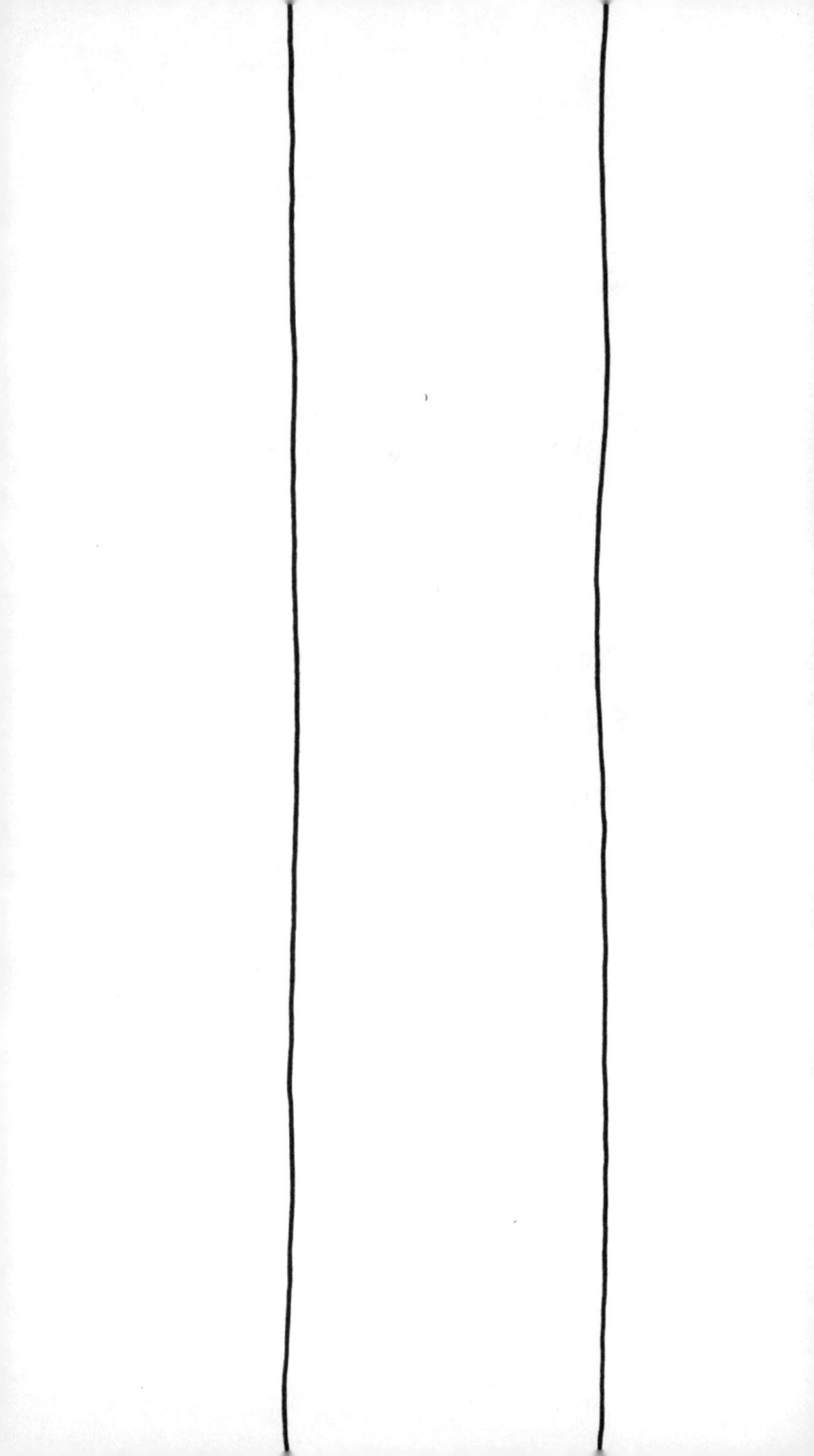

1.15

The compositional "rule of thirds" is universally harmonious, although harmony alone is not universally good. Too much discord isn't palatable; too much harmony is boring.

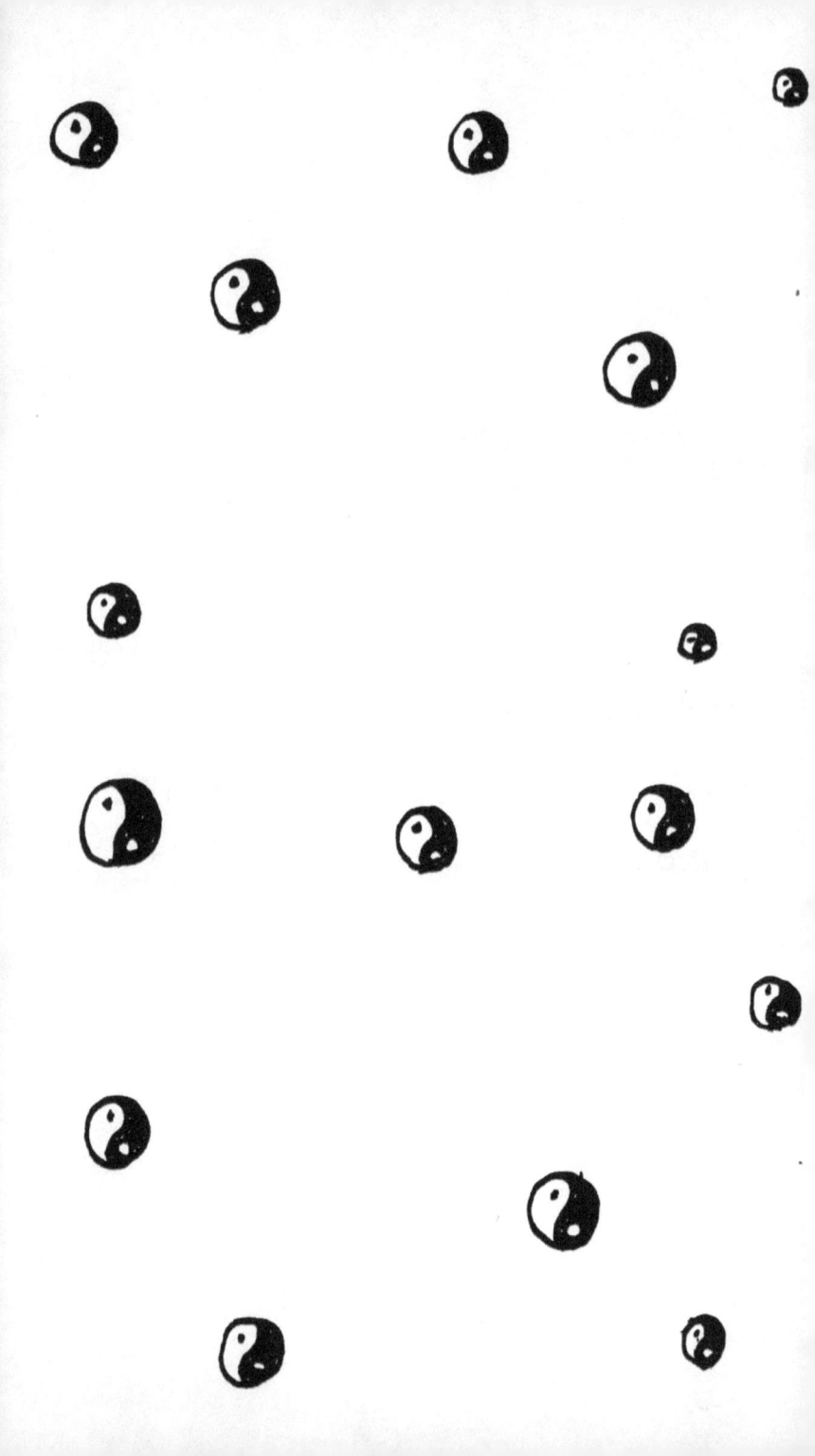

1.16

Contrast creates dynamic images, not just light with dark, but light-heartedness with deep subject matter, or complexity with big open spaces. How your elements contrast with each other are important relationships to consider.

CONTINUITY
BECAUSE IT'S ALL
BLACK LINE

1.17

Be conscious of when marks clash because they are from such different worlds that we lose believability. The world of photography is very different from the world of abstract shape. The world ballpoint pen evokes is different from the world of swirling "wet" paint. Coexistence is possible, but be careful to keep continuity between "voices"—— unless a jarring effect suits your intentions

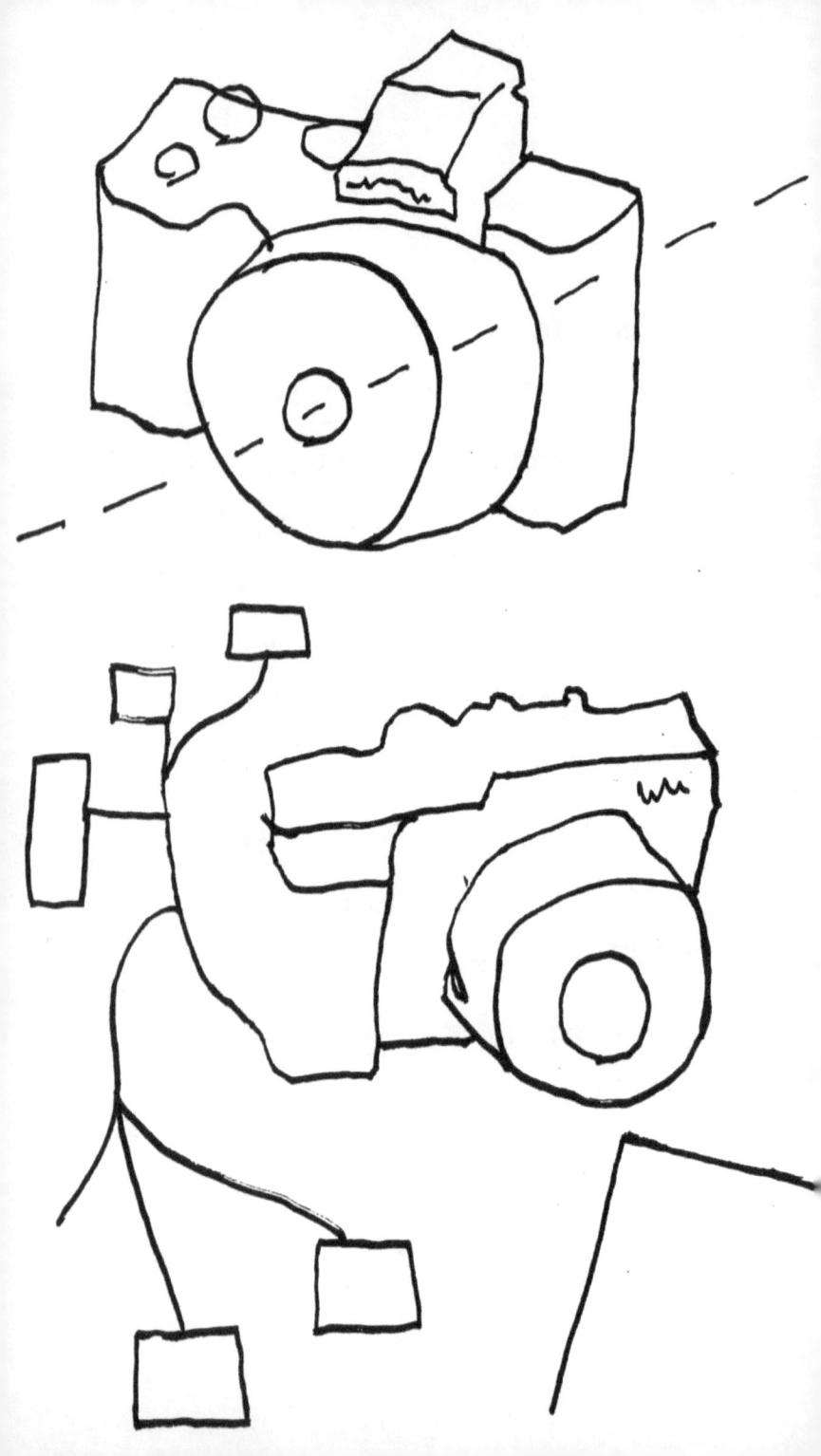

1.18

The more you understand your tools, the more able you are to choose ones that suit your objective(s)

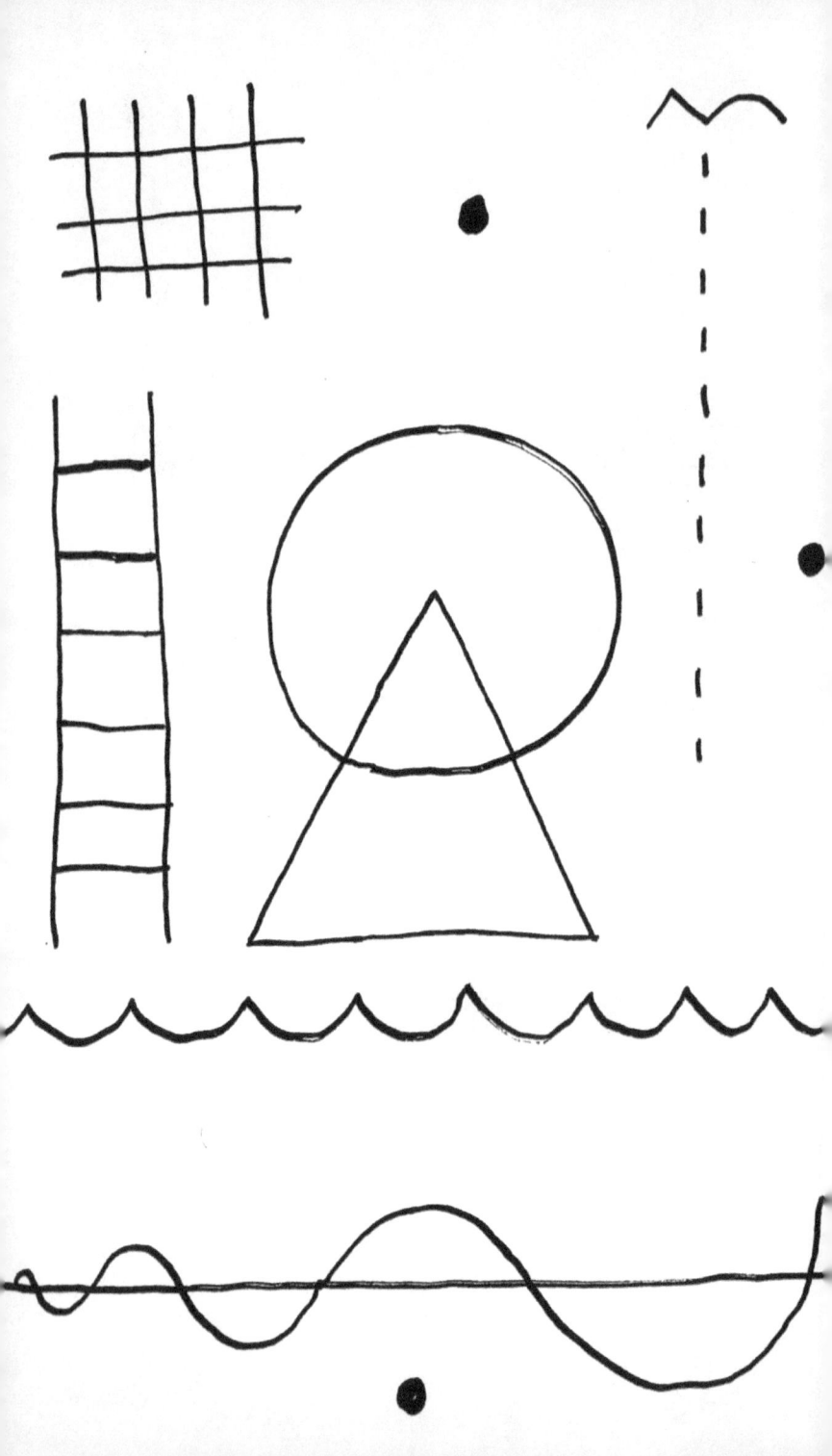

1.19

Everyone is creative in their own right. An engineer creates solutions while being bound by the laws of physics, translating designs and ideas into practical application. A cook creates dishes that have brief lives that sustain us, and are made by manipulating ingredients and refining recipes. A visual artist has alot of freedom within the visual realm. Although some creativity is useful, it isn't necessary to make something practical or useful when we're creative. We have space to speculate and demonstrate poetically without being committed to the reductive nature of a diagram. In a world that often requires solutions that say "this is that", a painting can be a great reprieve from utility. Where instruction isn't, there's room for viewers to create their own meaning.

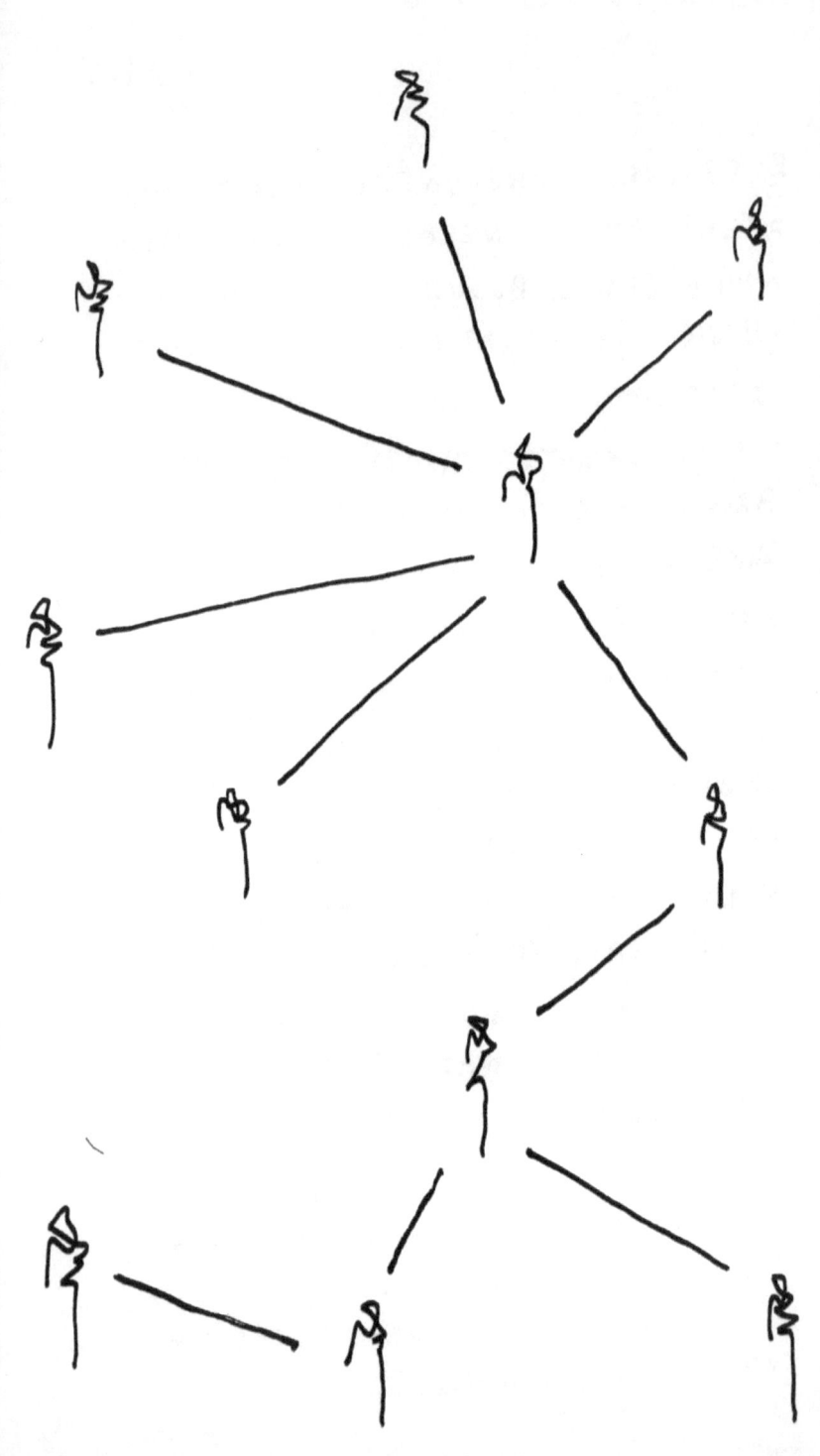

1.20

THE MOST DYNAMIC IMAGES DON'T IMPOSE OR DEFINE MEANING; THEY DESCRIBE AND LET VIEWERS DECIDE FOR THEMSELVES WHAT THOSE DESCRIPTIONS MEAN.

BEFORE...

A should go to B.

AFTER....

A went to C.

1.21

Showing your work makes you vulnerable because you can't completely control how your work is viewed. You're especially vulnerable when you have intentions, because since you have a goal you've said you'll fail if you don't reach it.

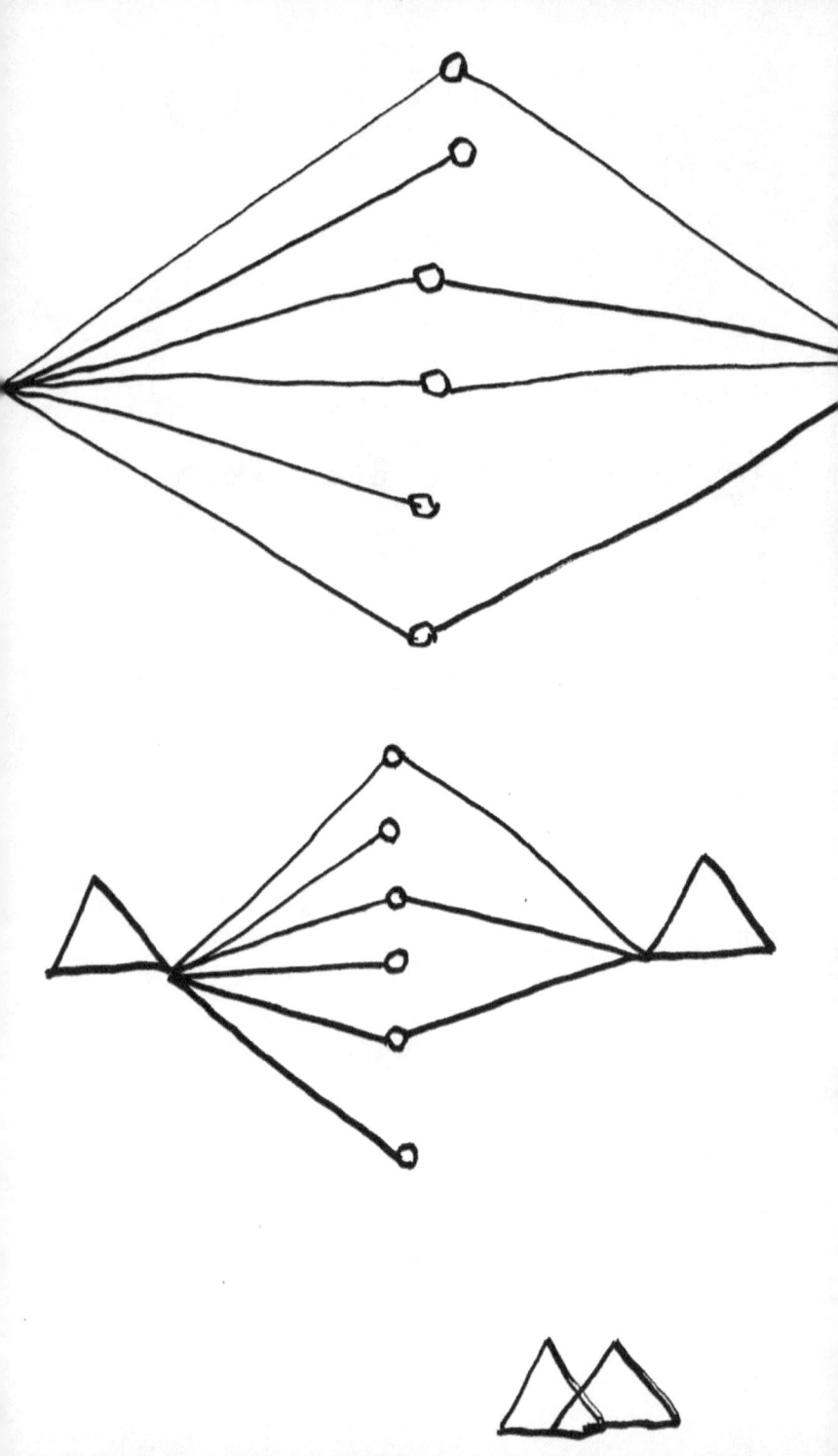

1.22

When you make a work of art, you do so with your own framework. The "viewer", if a separate person from the artist, has their own framework available, which has similarities and differences to yours. It is often the artists' job to make sure their work is accessible to viewers other than themselves, which may sound trivial, requires us to understand what is and isn't translating to other frameworks or points of view.

1.23

THINK ABOUT WHAT YOU'RE NOT SAYING, WHAT MARKS YOU'RE NOT MAKING.
WHAT ARE YOU SAYING BY OMISSION.

W? K? Q? L?
A? V? N? C? P?
F? X?
O? E?
M? T?
B? Y? Z?
D? H?
R?
S? I? J?
G? U?

1.24

It's possible to over-reflect or over-moderate. Sometimes the best choice in pursuing creativity is to distract yourself and think about something else. Grounding yourself by going for a walk can connect you to the realities of life.

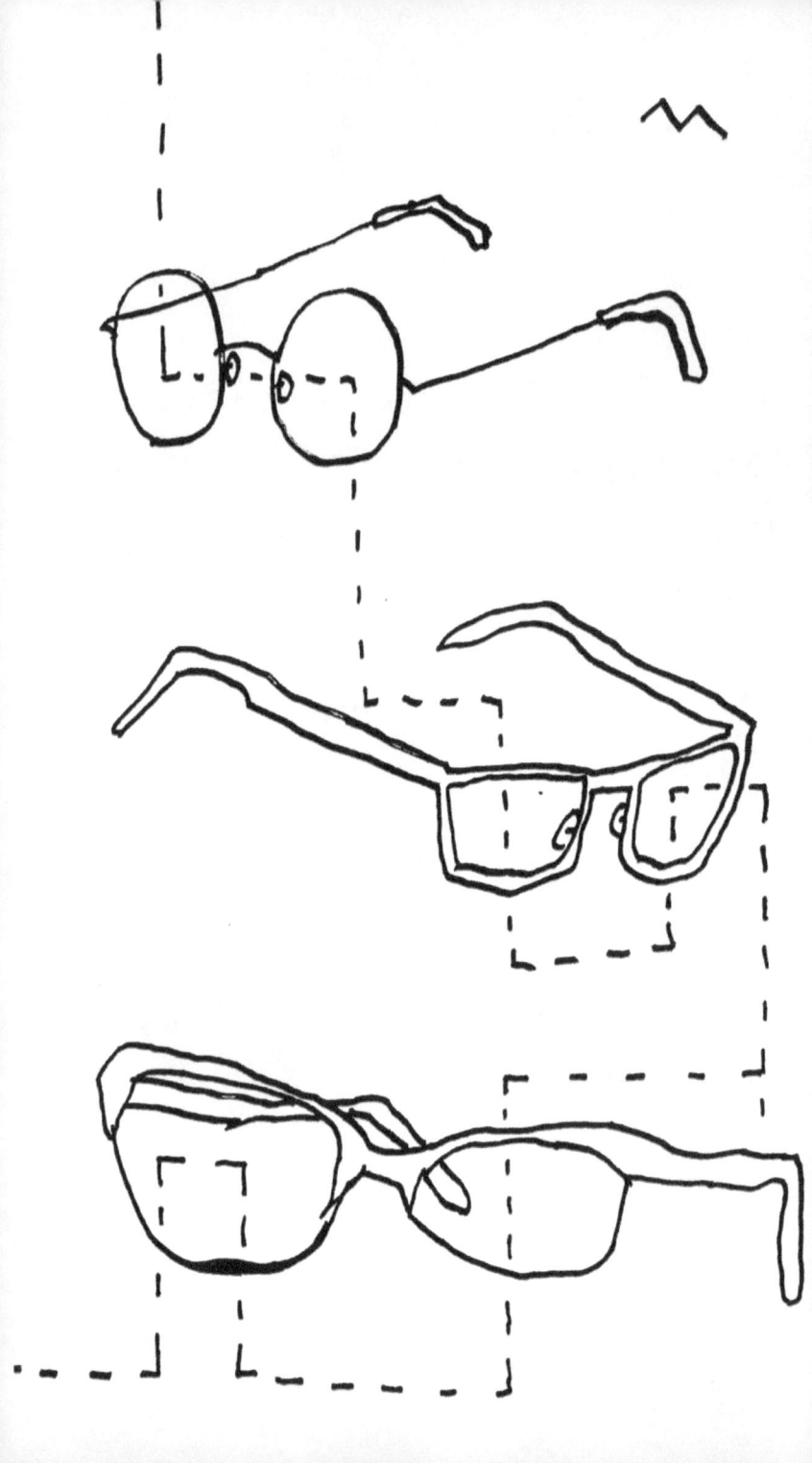

1.25

Get a good night's sleep. Although it may seem like this moment is the moment to control your art from, we benefit from making space between viewings as it facilitates a diverse perspective. After working on something all day it can be helpful to gain a "fresh set of eyes". When you view again you'll be doing so with a different bias, not without one. You'll see things differently, sometimes so much so, it might seem like the objects themselves have changed.

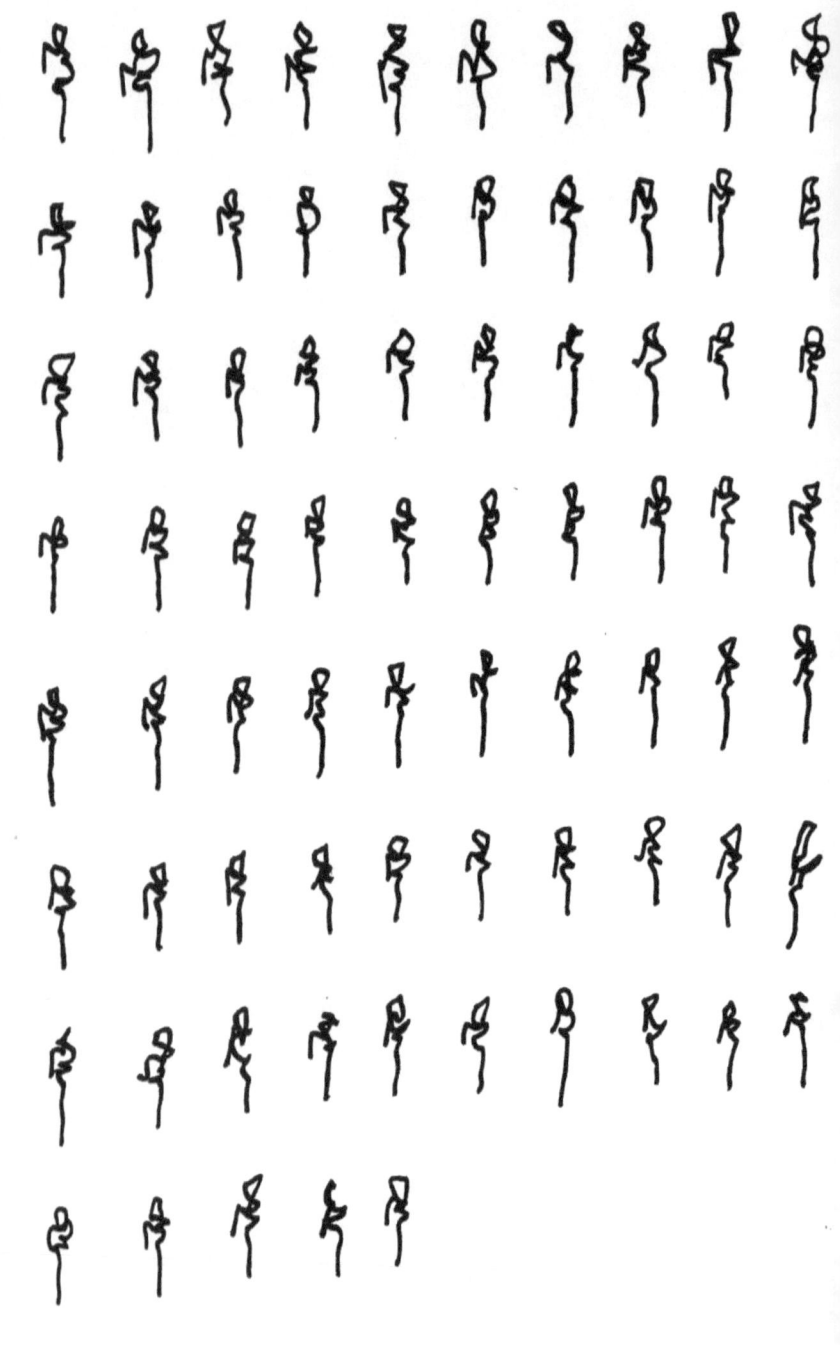

JOHN@JFGERRARD.COM

@JOHN_F_GERRARD

JOHNFGERRARD.COM

PORTFOLIO ↴

www.ingramcontent.com/pod-product-compliance
Lightning Source LLC
Chambersburg PA
CBHW030506220526
45464CB00006B/2677